CLEVELAND EMOTIONAL HEALTH

PROMOTING DISTINGUISHED
MENTAL HEALTH COUNSELING

Geneseo, N.Y.

clevelandemotionalhealth.com

ISBN Paperback: 9798990628403
ISBN Electronic: 9798990628410

Library of Congress Control Number: 2024908931

Disclaimer:
The content of this book is for informational purposes only and is intended to furnish readers with general information on matters that you may find to be of interest. The information that is provided in this book is not intended to replace or serve as a substitute for business, legal, ethical, or professional advice. The information that is provided in this book is not intended to replace or serve as a substitute for mental health treatment, medical treatment, or advice. As the reader of this book, you understand that the information contained in this book is not intended as a substitute for consultation or treatment with a licensed medical or mental health professional. Please consult with your own mental health counselor/therapist for your mental health needs. The reading and use of this book implies your acceptance of this disclaimer.

Printed in the United States of America.

MANDALAS

Throughout this book, you will encounter various mandalas to enjoy which serve as both a creative outlet for promoting mindfulness and inner calmness.

Mandalas are intricate geometric designs originating from ancient spiritual traditions, often symbolizing the universe's wholeness and unity. These circular patterns serve as a visual aid for meditation and contemplation, inviting individuals to focus their thoughts and find inner calmness. The repetitive and symmetrical nature of mandalas encourages a meditative state and a sense of harmony. Mandalas can be found across various cultures and spiritual practices, embodying diverse meanings and universally representing balance and interconnectedness.

Coloring mandalas has gained popularity as a therapeutic and creative activity with numerous mental health benefits. Engaging in the coloring process allows individuals to enter a mindful state, redirecting attention away from stressors and promoting relaxation. The act of choosing colors and filling in intricate patterns strengthens internal control and creativity. Coloring mandalas has been associated with reduced anxiety, increased focus, and improved mood. This meditative practice provides a constructive outlet for self-expression and can serve as a form of therapy to encourage a sense of joy and mindful awareness.

CONTENTS

> Take a moment and express your current thoughts, reflections, or any ideas that occupy your mind at this moment. Feel free to revisit this writing exercise as needed or whenever you wish.

> Explore my deepest motivation: What truly drives my need and desire to establish boundaries?

> Identify your values, what you are okay and not okay with.

> Write in detail about my principle values, what I am truly okay with and not okay with.

    Write about how I will communicate and
    implement my boundaries, both with yourself and
    others.

    Write about any comments, confusion, and
    questions that come to mind about setting my
    boundaries.

    Write about my reflections and what I have
    learned throughout this experience. Write any
    additional thoughts and ideas that arise.

~ 1 ~

GUIDING THE PEN

With a goal to extend the importance of setting boundaries to a wider audience, I find myself compelled to share insights on the transformative power of this practice.

In my counseling sessions, I am frequently discussing the misalignment between what you want, and what you are doing. This discrepancy often leads to considerable distress, and the inability to make personal choices within a framework of your values and limitations.

I cherish my role as a licensed mental health counselor, assisting members of rural communities in navigating their personal challenges. My intervention skills and techniques move beyond emphasizing only symptom reduction. Instead, my approach cultivates profound neural structural changes that facilitate genuine healing, therefore gaining sustainable transformations to reach the patient's desired goals.

During my doctoral training, I gravitated toward experiential psychodynamic, mindful, and strengths-based treatments and interventions. These interventions explore the interplay of unconscious and conscious awareness, childhood experiences, and how unresolved inner conflicts impact an individual's thoughts, behaviors patterns, and emotional well-being.

I am largely a geek who dedicates much of my free time to reading, writing, listening to podcasts, watching videos, and concentrating my continuing education on the inner workings of human behavior.

In my practice, I have learned that, despite our culture highlighting individual differences, I observe a connecting truth—the commonality in human mental struggles rather than their differences. This shared experience connects us more than you may realize.

Drawing on my experience as a seasoned mental health professional, I am dedicated to the work of healing, alleviating suffering, and helping individuals find meaning through the practice of kindness and compassion towards oneself and others. I endorse the importance of a work-life balance, prioritizing organization, self-structure, and intentional living over passive functioning.

I strongly believe that to effect desired change, regular practice of a new way of being is necessary and must be intentional. This intentional practice is crucial for any change to occur because repetition forms and reinforces new habits. Consistent practice helps rewire the brain's neural connections, solidifying desired behaviors and making them more automatic. Regular practice of desired change transforms it from a concept into a tangible and sustainable reality, enabling long-term growth and development.

The purpose of this book is to emphasize one aspect of mental well-being—setting boundaries for yourself—to enable a happier and more fulfilling life.

Everything I present here is integral to my personal practice, and I recognize the difficulties associated with long-term and sustainable change. The one thing I know for sure, is that intentional and purposeful effort, for any desired change, is essential for happiness, contentment, and healthy interpersonal relationships.

~ Catherine G. Cleveland

~ 2 ~
EXPRESSING YOURSELF IN WRITING

This book is designed to be written in. Why? Because the act of writing has a profound impact on the brain, influencing various *cognitive processes* and *neural pathways*.

Cognitive processes refer to the mental activities involved in acquiring, processing, storing, and using information. These processes include perception, attention, memory, language, problem-solving, decision-making, and reasoning. Cognitive processing is needed for learning, problem-solving, and adapting to new situations and lifestyle choices.

Neural pathways are connections formed by neurons (nerve cells) in the brain. These pathways enable the transmission of signals and information between different areas of the brain, allowing for communication and coordination of various functions. Each neural pathway is a series of connected neurons that work together to transmit specific types of information or facilitate particular actions. These pathways play a crucial role in various cognitive processes. The repeated use and reinforcement of neural pathways contribute to the brain's ability to adapt and learn, a phenomenon known as neural plasticity.

When you engage in the act of writing, you undergo a unique encoding process that contributes to improved memory and comprehension. Engaging in writing puts your thoughts into language which enhances your ability to generate ideas and improves problem solving skills.

Writing down your thoughts in this book strengthens the neural connections responsible for conscious versus unconscious attention. Conscious attention is crucial for well-being because it enables you to direct your mental resources towards healthy experiences, thoughts, and behaviors while effectively processing negative ones.

James Pennebaker, who is known for his theory of expressive writing, explains that expressing emotions through writing can have profound therapeutic effects. His research indicates that individuals who engage in expressive writing about emotional experiences will likely gain psychological benefits, such as connecting to, rather than avoiding your feelings—where avoiding your feelings is a type of dissociation. Dissociation, a type of unconsciousness, is a psychological defense mechanism where you disconnect from your thoughts, feelings, memories, or sense of identity, often as a response to trauma or overwhelming stress. Dissociation leads to a perceived detachment from the reality of the present moment.

While engaging in this process of self-reflection by writing in this book, you will tap into thoughts and feelings that you may have been avoiding for most of your life. This may trigger some physical and psychological discomfort, but it is crucial not to sidestep these emotions in order to initiate healing and achieve your desired goals.

Writing in a book offers several advantages, including:

- **Active Engagement:** Writing in this book will actively engage your mind, enhancing your mental processing and retention of information compared to just reading alone.

- **Personalization:** This book encourages writing about your personal ideas, reflections, and annotations, enabling a customized learning experience tailored to your needs. Try your best to write without the voice of the negative internal critic—this is an important skill to develop.

- **Visual Reinforcement:** Writing reinforces visual learning. Seeing your own words can aid in mental processing, memory recall, and conceptual clarification.

- **Organization:** This book provides a semi-structured format, helping you organize information in a logical manner, making it easier to review and revisit later.

- **Self-Paced Learning** (my favorite)**:** Self-paced writing allows you to progress at your own pace, promoting concentration, abstract concepts, and deep reflection.

- **Skill Development:** Even if you dislike writing, it can improve your writing skills, critical thinking, and problem-solving abilities.

- **Memory Enhancement:** The act of recalling information by writing reinforces learning through retrieval practice, contributing to long-term memory retention.

As you will notice, writing in this book actively involves you in the learning process, thus contributing to a more effective and personalized learning experience.

After each chapter, you will find dedicated space to write down your reflections and thoughts. Each writing section includes a prompt, but also feel free to express anything that comes to mind. Write freely, there are no rules. Practice keeping your inner critic (your superego) in check and focus on simply writing—let your thoughts flow onto the page without inhibition. Write, write, and write some more.

Please note, that there is no need to express all your thoughts at once. Dedicate moments throughout the day to contemplate what boundaries holds significance for you. When an idea or thought spontaneously occurs, I recommend writing it down promptly, as thoughts and ideas can vanish as swiftly as they emerge.

Consider keeping this book handy at all times for your convenience. It provides ample space to document your thoughts, ideas, and plans. If someone else happens to notice this book while in your possession, it could have two potential effects.

First, they might connect with you and express, "That's great, I need to set boundaries too!" Alternatively, they might distance themselves, recognizing that you are prioritizing your self-worth and well-being by no longer tolerating manipulation or abuse from others.

Most importantly, listen deeply and intentionally to what is emerging from your soul. This is about you!

Writing Exercises

Pause after each chapter in this book to reflect on what you are learning. Reread as needed. We all learn at our own pace. Use the expressive writing prompts to actively involve and inspire your introspection.

Engaging in introspection is the process of examining and reflecting upon your thoughts, feelings, and experiences, with the intentional aim of gaining deeper self-understanding and insight.

Exercise A ~ Take a moment and express your current thoughts, reflections, or any ideas that occupy your mind at this moment. Feel free to revisit this writing exercise as needed or whenever you wish (p. 11).

Exercise B ~ Explore my deepest motivation: what truly drives my need and desire to establish boundaries (p. 20)?

Exercise C ~ Write in detail about my principle values, what I am truly okay with and not okay with (p. 29).

Exercise D ~ Make a list of boundaries that I want to put in place for my mental well-being (p.42).

Exercise E ~ Write down consequences that appropriately align with my boundaries (p. 54).

Exercise F ~ Write about the various facets of emotions, behaviors, or sabotage that emerge when I am contemplating and/or establishing my boundaries (p. 76).

Exercise G ~ Write about how I will communicate and implement my boundaries, both with yourself and others (p. 97).

Exercise H ~ Write about any comments, confusion, and questions that come to mind about setting my boundaries (p. 111).

Exercise I ~ Write about my reflections and what I have learned throughout this experience. Write any additional thoughts and ideas that arise (p. 123)

~ A ~

Take a moment and express your current thoughts, reflections, or any ideas that occupy your mind at this moment. Feel free to revisit this writing exercise as needed or whenever you wish.

~ 3 ~
SETTING BOUNDARIES

The renowned emotions researcher, author, and professor, Brené Brown, defines boundaries as "what is okay and what is not okay." Her research data explains that boundaries are about respect for yourself, and for the other person.

When boundaries are absent, the clear lines in a relationship can become fuzzy, leading to a situation where you might end up shouldering responsibilities that rightfully belong to someone else.

Over time, these blurred lines can cause anger and resentment, affecting your ability to be compassionate. Brown underscores that nothing of true value can be sustained without boundaries. She advocates for the ability to be straightforward about what is acceptable to you while upholding a spirit of love and generosity.

Boundaries are personal and originate from your values, manifesting as physical, emotional, and mental limits. These limits are established to protect yourself from manipulation, abuse, or violation by others.

People sometimes make the mistake of blaming others for their inability to set and implement boundaries. However, boundaries are set, implemented, and maintained by you!

Establishing and maintaining healthy, personalized boundaries is crucial for your self-respect, self-confidence, mental health, and cultivating kind and caring interpersonal relationships.

The process of setting boundaries involves clearly communicating your needs, desires, and limits, starting with yourself and then with others. Without boundaries, your life is likely to be marked by persistent anger and resentment towards others, as well as disrespect for yourself.

THE FOUR ESSENTIAL PILLARS
FOR SETTING YOUR BOUNDARIES

A pillar is a structural element that serves as a vertical support, typically designed to bear a load and provide stability to a structure.

In psychological terms, a pillar is a fundamental construct that provides essential cognitive or emotional support and stability for your mental well-being. Just as architectural pillars bear the weight of a structure, psychological pillars bear the cognitive and emotional load, offering a sense of security, empowerment, and self-worth. The foundational aspects of boundary setting, represented by these four pillars, offer necessary support as you commence into this transformative journey.

- **Pillar 1 Identifying Values** ~ Values are what your are okay with and not okay with and they align with your principles and beliefs.

- **Pillar 2 Setting Boundaries** ~ Understand that boundaries are for you, not against others; and when crossed, you are the one who crosses them.

- **Pillar 3 Incorporating Consequences** ~ Boundaries must have appropriately matching consequences.

- **Pillar 4 Addressing Emotions, Behaviors, and Self-Sabotage** ~ It is important to address the internal landscape of emotional responses that arise, sabotaging your well intentioned boundary and consequence setting.

~B~

Explore my deepest motivation: what truly drives my need and desire to establish boundaries?

~ 4 ~
PILLAR 1

IDENTIFYING VALUES

Begin by identifying your values. Values are what you are okay with and not okay with that align with your principles and beliefs. This process is a very personal journey. Be mindful of the "should" thoughts —what I think other people think I should be doing. These thoughts arise from your negative internal critic. Instead, approach this process with kindness, by reaching deeper, and listening to your soul—the truly authentic you.

It is interesting, that as children we easily knew what we liked and what we did not like— "I like blue, not red". However, through the process of maturing and forced external cultural demands, we tend to be more concerned with others' opinions as we become more identified with the need to be liked and not judged. Consequently, as adults, we (unconsciously) become detached from our core values—what we are truly okay with and what we are not okay with.

Here are some examples to get you started identifying your values:

- I know for sure that I like working for myself and prefer to be self-structured.

- Or, I prefer to have more structure in my life rather than have the stress of higher level decision making.

- My sleep is very important to my well-being, so I am choosing to be on a consistent sleep schedule.

- Being in nature is important to me.

- I don't like being around you when you are drinking.

- I am not okay with my boss (or anyone) who talks down to me, shames, or guilts me.

- I am not okay when someone makes me feel bad when I have done nothing wrong.

- I don't like how often I automatically say "I'm sorry."

- Healthy eating and nutrition are important to me and I want to stay true to this value.

- Sometimes I get over isolated and need to socialize more to feel more balanced.

- Or, sometimes I feel over socialized and I am avoiding myself instead of feeding my soul.

- I notice that I let people manipulate me, and I don't want to let that happen any more.

- I want to be kinder and more compassionate to myself and to others.

- My social activities outside of work and family are important to me (skiing, golf, book club, yoga, etc).

- I am not okay when I let my work guilt me into more hours than my compliance contract requires.

- Helping others is a necessary part of my life.

- I do not want to raise helpless and entitled children.

- It is important to me to maintain a sustainable and healthy lifestyle.

- It drives me crazy when people show up late to important gatherings.

- I am a grown adult, and I don't like that my parent(s) can still be overbearing.

- I want to stop asking my spouse permission to live my best life.

- It's beginning to bother me hanging out with my friends who are partying too much.

Observe that these examples reflect genuine truths, and the objective is to evolve into a more authentic version of yourself. The repercussions of not being genuine with your values include feelings of anger and resentment. This emotional response often surfaces in reaction to others' behaviors, stemming from your lack of personal boundaries.

Additionally, not being clear on your values can manifest internally as self-loathing and self-deprecation, indicative of low self-worth and limited self-confidence. Such internal struggles are contraindicated to achieving happiness and contentment. Remember to refrain from shaming or negatively judging your values, and be mindful that they do not cause harm to others.

~C~

Write in detail about my principle values, what I am truly okay with and not okay with.

~ 5 ~
Pillar 2

SETTING BOUNDARIES

Understand that boundaries are for you, not against others; and when crossed, you are the one who crosses them. It is crucial to recognize that boundaries are derived from your values and are set in place for you. When counseling patients, I often encounter statements such as, "I had that boundary with _____, but they keep crossing it."

Consider boundaries from this perspective: they are a reflection of my values, indicating what aligns with my comfort or discomfort. If my boundaries are breached, it is essential to understand that I am the one who—consciously or unconsciously—crosses them. Understanding this concept highlights the importance of taking personal responsibility for keeping and strengthening boundaries that match your values.

The great thing about setting boundaries is that they are yours— unique to you. You can keep them forever or change them at any time. Use your wisdom and experience to establish the boundaries essential for your happiness and contentment, steering clear of a lifetime filled with frustration, disrespect, and unhappiness.

In addition to setting interpersonal boundaries—boundaries relating to others—it is necessary to set inner-personal boundaries as well. Inner-personal boundaries refer to the emotional and psychological limits you establish within yourself to promote a healthy and happy life. These boundaries act as your guiding principles, stemming from self-awareness, recognizing personal needs, and tuning into your emotional responses.

Setting healthy inner-personal boundaries involves mindful and nonjudgmental internal dialogues that promote self-observation and self-connectedness, establishing a foundation for self-confidence and self-worth.

As well as establishing and maintaining interpersonal boundaries, inner-personal boundaries are crucial for several reasons. Your inner-personal boundaries help safeguard your mental health by preventing excessive self-criticism, burnout, unnecessary chronic mental problems, and physical suffering. These personalized boundaries allow for a clearer understanding of your needs and goals to become the best version of you—the phenomenon that you are.

To reiterate, absence of inner-personal boundaries can pave the way for succumbing to the adverse effects of lifestyle diseases. Establishing guidelines for yourself becomes a pivotal defense, fortifying against the potential health challenges associated with today's unhealthy standard of living.

.

Here are examples of some of boundaries to help get you started:

- Exercise must be a part of my weekly routine.

- If I am in an abusive relationship, how am I accountable (if I don't like the clown's behavior, why is it I keep going to the circus?).

- I will no longer make excuses for your antisocial public behaviors.

- I will not respond to (staying silent) or engage in manipulative questions or judgmental remarks.

- I am okay with saying "no" repeatedly, or repeating my answer verbatim when someone is not accepting my response.

- Everyday, I will give undivided attention (put the phone down) to my kids, spouse, pets, etc.

- I will practice mindful self-observation daily without the use of shameful self-judgment. I am a work in progress.

- I am not responsible for taking care of someone else's negative emotions (unless they are your children).

- I accept that you are not going to give up your alcohol. However, if you are drunk and slurring your words, I will leave as soon as I arrive (said an adult daughter to her mother).

~D~

Make a list of boundaries that I want to put in place for my mental well-being.

~ 6 ~
Pillar 3

INCORPORATING CONSEQUENCES

Meaningful boundaries are established when they are accompanied by appropriately matching consequences. Without having explicitly stated consequences, you will have outcomes which are likely not in your favor. Therefore, ensure that you are clear and intentional in expressing your consequences and that they align with your boundaries.

For instance, my boundary is: "If you cheat on me," a fitting consequence is: "I will end the relationship." However, if someone disrupts my exercise time, leaving them is excessive, and the consequence does not align appropriately.

You will notice that certain boundaries are firm, while others offer flexibility—it is your decision. You will also notice that if there are no consequences for your boundaries, the result will be feelings of anger, frustration, and resentment mostly toward others, but also toward yourself.

Again, consequences play a vital role; without them, a boundary loses its effectiveness. The absence of consequences can lead to adverse outcomes for you, due to your inaction. Remember to be kind to yourself in this process.

If, however, you are setting boundaries for yourself, the associated consequences are already in place. For example, if you choose to eat a healthy, non-processed food diet, and you cross this boundary, the consequence is poor health and the potential for chronic discomfort and disease.

It is widely recognized that lacking inner-personal boundaries can create a detrimental synergy that cripples both mental and physical health. For example, habits like a sedentary lifestyle, unhealthy diet, inadequate sleep, substance use, and chronic stress will collectively contribute to a cascade of negative effects.

Physically, they can lead to chronic pain, weakened immune function, and an increased risk of chronic diseases. Living in this unconscious or mindless lifestyle can also have negative implications for mental health, such as different types of anxiety, hopelessness, and low self-worth.

This intricate connection between the mind and body means that compromised physical health can exacerbate mental health challenges, and vice versa. Breaking the cycle requires an intentional desire, emphasizing the importance of living a balanced life. On the other hand, it is important to recognize that within you, there may be a reluctance to alter what feels familiar. These opposing forces can trigger an internal battle that can be severely distressing and may require external support.

This is why it is essential to be clear about your values: what I am okay with, and what I am not okay with (Pillar 1), and write down the boundaries you need to have in place (Pillar 2). In doing so, you embrace the authentic you while cultivating kindness and compassion, both for yourself and others.

As you are discovering, you cannot embody love and kindness without having your boundaries in place along with their matching consequences.

~E~

Write down consequences that appropriately align with my boundaries.

~ 7 ~
Pillar 4

ADDRESSING EMOTIONS,
BEHAVIORS, AND SELF-SABOTAGE

Here, we take a peek at the internal landscape of emotional responses that arise, sabotaging your well intentioned boundary and consequence setting. If you have ever attempted to establish boundaries, you may have noticed how specific emotions and behaviors can hinder your progress. These obstacles need to be addressed to overcome the challenges inhibiting your goals.

Guilt

One of the most common feelings associated with boundary setting is guilt. Guilt is a combination of physiological and psychological experiences that arise when you have done something wrong. If you find yourself in the wrong, it is normal to feel a sense of remorse and is important to address the situation through repair or a sincere apology.

However, guilt can suddenly appear with a forceful energy whenever you decide to set an intention to take care of your well-being. For instance, guilt can appear when initiating a meditation practice or trying to dedicate some alone time, when family, social, or work demands are pulling at your attention.

Experiencing guilt of this nature can manifest physical discomfort, as your mind persistently signals a sense of wrongdoing. You may not be consciously aware of how frequently these occurrences are happening.

Interestingly, this type of guilt is not authentic; instead, it is a form of self-punishment rooted in lifelong internalization of external influences. It is important to distinguish between genuine remorse and the unwarranted burden of guilt imposed by external expectations—"what I should be doing"—allowing for a more authentic and self-compassionate approach to understanding your values.

Shame

Shame, on the other hand is a complex and powerful emotion characterized by feelings of unworthiness, humiliation, or disgrace. It can lead to negative self-image, self-loathing, and intrusive thoughts. Unlike guilt, which is focused on actions, shame centers on self-worth, resulting in feeling unaccomplished in life due to a desire to conceal perceived flaws or mistakes.

Here are several instances illustrating the harmful inner-voice and sometimes behaviors associated with guilt and shame:

- Setting boundaries makes me feel selfish (I am bad).

- My values are not as important as it is to please you.

- I am afraid to set boundaries.

- I stay in unhealthy relationships.

- I stay in a job I dread.

- I am not living up to my values.

- I apologize when I have done nothing wrong.

- I do what is expected rather than following my dreams.

- I tell people what I want them to hear rather than speak my truth.

- I avoid feeling my emotions.

- I call myself names like stupid and lazy.

- I frequently seek external validation as a gauge of my self-worth.

- I do not feel confident in several areas of my life.

This punishing guilt and shame can be profound and unsettling, creating chronic inner-conflict. One part of us yearns for self-established boundaries to break free from the cycle of anger, resentment, and destructive relating. While, another part of us wrestles with the idea that establishing boundaries is seen as wrong. As described by acclaimed peer counselor and speaker Dawn Reckahn-Stone, self-avoidance tendencies triggers default behaviors such as "going along to get along" which can exacerbate conditions, such as anxiety, to the point of becoming a panic attack.

Helplessness

When guilt and shame become too overpowering, a helpless mentality can form in some individuals. A helpless mentality is a mindset characterized by a sense of powerlessness or a belief that one lacks control over their circumstances.

Individuals with a helpless mentality may perceive challenges as insurmountable, leading to a passive approach in dealing with difficulties. This mindset can restrict adaptive problem-solving skills and strategies.

This way of being can also manifest as passive-aggressive behavior when individuals, feeling powerless, express their frustration or resistance indirectly. The underlying sense of helplessness contributes to a cycle of indirect expression of negative feelings, making it challenging to address issues openly and constructively.

Rather than openly addressing concerns, one may resort to subtle forms of resistance, sarcasm, projection, or avoidance. These passive-aggressive tendencies can create tension in relationships, as it obstructs clear communication and accountability for one's actions.

Blaming

Another way that people remove themselves from the psychological pain of guilt and shame is by adapting a blaming mentality of, "Why is this happening to me?" A blaming mentality is a mindset characterized by a propensity to attribute faults or responsibility for problems to others or events rather than accepting personal accountability. Individuals with a blaming mentality typically focus on external factors as the cause of their difficulties, purposely and unconsciously avoiding introspection or self-reflection.

Fear and Worry

When it comes to why you undermine your values and boundaries, the predominant worry often revolves around the need for being liked by others and the fear of being perceived negatively. This leads you to the realization that letting go and moving on from toxic relationships is sometimes imperative, but is also a fearful process that can leave you with feelings of loneliness, isolation, and being unwanted.

Releasing the addictive grasp for external validation, the need to be liked or approved of, allows space for cultivating healthy internal validation through self-kindness. This encourages enhancements in creativity, goal-setting, self-confidence, and consequently, nurtures a sense of authenticity and fulfilling empowerment.

When difficult times happen, recognize that suffering is inherent to the human experience, an inevitable aspect of being alive. Guard against adopting a victim mentality by acknowledging that challenging and sometimes painful situations occur regularly. In most cases, these occurrences are not personally targeted at you; neither God nor the universe is conspiring against you. Embrace the perspective that things are "happening", not "happening to you." This mindset helps avoid adding suffering to unavoidable suffering, or unnecessarily creating drama, and drama is never appropriate.

Self-Sabotage

Self-sabotage is a complex and counterproductive pattern of behavior where individuals undermine their own success, well-being, or goals and is often created by a lack of self-confidence and self-kindness. Self-sabotage involves unconscious actions or thoughts that compromise personal growth and achievement. This self-destructive behavior can manifest in various forms, such as procrastination, negative self-talk, fear of success, or engaging in harmful habits.

The underlying causes of self-sabotage are rooted in deep-seated cultural beliefs, past traumas, guilt, and shame. Breaking free from the cycle of self-sabotage requires self-awareness, introspection, and a commitment to intentional change.

Pay mindful attention to how often you put yourself down, put labels on yourself such as stupid or other deprecating terms, the tone in which you address yourself, and the behaviors you incorporate to not take care of your well-being. For instance, using substances or pharmaceuticals to numb out, avoiding your emotions, not being kind, not utilizing your creative soul, or not having a tidy space to work and live in.

Self-Deprecation

Self-deprecating behaviors involve consistently belittling or undervaluing yourself, expressed through negative self-talk, minimizing achievements, or downplaying your self-worth. These behaviors can have detrimental effects on your confidence, while hindering personal growth and healthy connections with others.

Take time to observe the frequency of your self-criticism, the labels you attach to yourself, and the tone used in addressing yourself.

Pay attention to your self-deprecating behaviors like avoiding emotional expression, neglecting goal setting and creative pursuits, excessive procrastination, ignoring clutter and chaos in your living and work spaces, and using substances and pharmaceuticals to numb emotions.

Engaging with Narcissistic Behaviors

Narcissistic behaviors refer to patterns of exaggerated self-importance, a need for unhealthy attention, and a lack of empathy towards others. Individuals displaying these behaviors can easily justify their thoughts and actions, display blaming and helpless mentalities, and exploit interpersonal relationships for personal gain.

Healthy boundaries can be taken as criticism which is challenging terrain for narcissists, triggering defensive, angry, or passive-aggressive reactions as they struggle to accept their faults. In social and interpersonal interactions, a pattern of interrupting emerges, with narcissists frequently steering conversations back to themselves, showcasing a self-centered communication style. When these characteristics become persistent, they impair mental and social functioning.

How do you know you are encountering narcissistic behaviors? The signs include making you feel bad when you
have done nothing wrong, manipulating you to do things that go against your core values, disrespecting your time, you cannot explain their behavior with logic, and experiencing abuse in any form—whether emotional, intellectual, physical, or sexual.

Love or sex bombing is also narcissistic tactic where someone overwhelms another person with excessive affection, praise, offering sex, or constant attention in order to gain control or manipulate you emotionally. Love or sex bombing often occurs early in a relationship and can be a red flag for unhealthy dynamics, and the prompt execution of boundaries is essential.

Interacting with the narcissistic individual is a difficult population when it comes to setting boundaries. Therefore, it is crucial to refrain from engaging, by explaining your position with the narcissistic personality. You know you are engaging when you feel the need to explain what is wrong with their behaviors, over and over again.

If you find yourself repeatedly explaining your position, you are essentially "parenting" them by exerting more effort, and they find satisfaction in witnessing your distress. Essentially, you are explaining proper behaviors to an adult, who already knows what you are explaining. Stop explaining yourself—this is a boundary. Explaining your position feeds their ego and they revel in it—don't do it!

Quality of Sleep

The quality of sleep is one of the most important aspects of your life, while playing a pivotal role in achieving personal and interpersonal goals. Sleep is a critical factor in overall well-being, encompassing physical health, cognitive functioning, and emotional stability. Adequate and restorative sleep contributes to enhanced concentration, memory consolidation, and optimal immune system functioning.

Sleep deprivation or poor sleep quality can sabotage goals by impairing cognitive function, reducing focus, and hindering effective decision-making. Moreover, the impact on mood and intensified emotions due to inadequate sleep can adversely affect your quality of life.

Prioritizing quality sleep is integral for sustaining both individual goals and nurturing healthy relationships. Chronic sleep deprivation is associated with an increased risk of various health issues, including cardiovascular diseases, obesity, and susceptibility to viruses. Emotionally, inadequate sleep can contribute to mood disturbances, and an increased propensity to mental health disorders.

Circadian rhythms, the natural internal cycles that regulate various physiological processes, play a crucial role in orchestrating the ebb and flow of our daily biological activities. They are an internal process that regulate the sleep-wake cycle and repeat roughly every 24 hours. Governed by the body's internal clock, these rhythms influence various physiological and behavioral changes, such as fluctuations in alertness, body temperature, and hormone production.

Exposure to light and darkness, particularly natural light cues first thing in the morning, helps synchronize the circadian rhythms to the external environment. Disruptions to these rhythms, for instance, due to irregular sleep patterns or shift work, can impact overall health. Understanding and aligning activities with circadian rhythms can contribute to improved health and functioning.

Likewise, mindful meditation practices will enhance sleep quality through various mechanisms. Firstly, it promotes relaxation and reduces anxiety, and lowers cortisol levels associated with sleep disturbances. Additionally, meditation encourages mindfulness, helping individuals detach from racing thoughts and quiet the mind, which is beneficial for overcoming insomnia. Regular meditation has been linked to increased production of melatonin, a hormone crucial for regulating sleep-wake cycles. Moreover, incorporating a consistent meditation practice creates an optimal mental state for falling asleep and maintaining restful sleep throughout the night.

Self-Kindness

Self-kindness is what replaces ruminating, worrying, and self-sabotage. Known for her groundbreaking work in compassion research, Kristin Neff posits that treating yourself with love and kindness is a pivotal aspect of healing from any suffering. Self-kindness involves treating oneself with warmth and understanding, particularly in the face of challenges or setbacks.

This aspect of self-compassion encourages individuals to replace self-criticism with a more nurturing and supportive inner-dialogue. What's more, Neff emphasizes the importance of extending the same kindness to oneself that one might naturally offer to a friend, creating a positive and compassionate relationship with your own experiences and emotions—in other words, be your own best friend.

For instance, when you recognize that you are not being kind to yourself, take a moment to appreciate your awareness—it is a commendable first step towards positive change. The next step involves acknowledging your actions without judgment or self-blame. Then, inquire within: "How can I treat myself more compassionately instead of resorting to self-shaming?" Even if you think you don't know how to be kind to yourself, you do. Extend the same comforting words to yourself as you would to a cherished friend or child in need of understanding and compassion.

With the absence of self-kindness, you risk a lifetime steeped in regret and persistent discontent, as your hopes and dreams—the desires of your soul—remain unaddressed and unfulfilled.

Being Your True and Authentic Self

Your true authentic self refers to the kindest and most genuine expression of who you are, free from external influences or societal expectations. True authenticity encompasses your core beliefs, values, and individuation (embracing your true and whole self—Carl

73

Jung) without conforming to external pressures.

Acknowledge that you are a unique phenomenon that possesses a true and authentic self. Discovering this entails tuning into yourself and practicing mindful self-observation. Simultaneously, practice disengaging from egoic behaviors that are self-centered and detrimental to both you and others.

Recognizing that cultivating self-worth is an ongoing practice that has a transformative nature, highlighting that your value extends beyond external validations. It involves embracing who you are at your core. This personal connection with self-worth and self-kindness can serve as the cornerstone for your emotional well-being and good mental health.

In summary, the intricate interplay between emotions, behaviors, and the potential for self-sabotage significantly influences the establishment and maintenance of your boundaries. Emotions can guide responses, and behaviors can express these emotional cues, creating a risk of self-sabotage when unaddressed. Recognizing this dynamic is crucial for self-worth and implementing strategies for effective boundary-setting.

Seeking guidance from a qualified mental health professional may be necessary in navigating this journey especially if you are committed to cultivating a healthier, balanced interpersonal and inner-personal connections.

~F~

Write about the various facets of emotions, behaviors, or sabotage that emerge when I am contemplating and/or establishing my boundaries.

~ 8 ~

COMMUNICATING MY BOUNDARIES

Effectively communicating boundaries requires clarity, assertiveness, and respect. Start by reviewing your thoughts from each writing exercise to ensure a clear understanding and confidence with your values, boundaries, and consequences.

INTERPERSONAL BOUNDARIES

When expressing interpersonal boundaries, use "I" statements to convey your feelings and needs without placing blame. Be direct and specific, avoiding vague language. If possible, choose an appropriate time and setting for the conversation, where both parties are in a receptive state. Maintain a calm and composed demeanor, emphasizing the importance of mutual respect. Encourage open dialogue, allowing the other person to express their perspective and ensuring a collaborative approach to establishing and maintaining your boundaries.

Implementing boundaries can be daunting and takes courage because it involves stepping into the unfamiliar territory to assert your needs and limits. You will be working within the fear that arises from concerns about potential conflict, rejection, or upsetting established dynamics in relationships.

Bear in mind that setting boundaries takes courage, and courage and comfort do not coexist, particularly in emotionally difficult situations, where courage requires stepping outside your comfort zone. When you are implementing your boundaries, there is an inherent vulnerability when expressing what is okay and not okay, and the fear rising in you can create anxiety and acute physical discomfort.

Some of the more difficult boundaries you have decided on require embracing the unknown, making the process of implementing boundaries feel overwhelming. Despite the initial fear, recognizing that boundaries are essential for quality relationships and well-being can provide some of the courage needed to navigate through this fear. Consider reaching out to a licensed mental health professional for assistance in navigating through these sometimes arduous endeavors.

Exercise caution when finding the need to explain yourself when dealing with individuals exhibiting narcissistic behaviors (review pages 69-71). If you find yourself repeatedly explaining your position, you inadvertently assume the role of teaching an adult what they already know. Reserve explanations for instances necessitating actual instruction, such as sharing new information or engaging in teaching moments with cognitively developing individuals, for example, children.

Remember, in this transformative process, to practice kindness towards yourself. Understand that mistakes will occur, and adjustments are a necessary part of this ongoing process—for we are all a work in progress.

INNER-PERSONAL BOUNDARIES

Implementing inner-personal boundaries involves a conscious and intentional process. Here are some steps to consider:

- **Self-Reflection** ~ Take time to reflect on your emotions, thoughts, and values from each writing exercise. Understand what matters to you and identify areas where you may need to establish your inner-personal boundaries.

- **Identify Any Physical Discomfort** ~ Recognize any situations or interactions that trigger emotional responses, since every emotion is felt physically in your body. This awareness helps you pinpoint where you might need to set boundaries to protect your well-being.

- **Communicate With Yourself** ~ Have honest and open internal dialogues. At times, doing this out loud can enhance its effectiveness. Acknowledge your needs and be clear about what is acceptable and unacceptable in terms of your inner experiences.

- **Be Truthful** ~ Explore your soul instead of yielding to ego-driven expectations—what I "should" be doing— to ensure authenticity in recognizing your genuine desires.

- **Establish Limits** ~ Define limits on any self-criticism, negative self-talk, or perfectionistic tendencies. These behaviors serve as indicators of deep-seated shame. Setting realistic expectations for yourself contributes to maintaining inner-personal boundaries.

- **Be Kind** ~ Nurture yourself with love and kindness, creating an environment that elevates both your self-worth and self-confidence.

- **Seek Support** ~ Talk to friends, family, clergy, spiritual teachers, or a mental health professional as needed. Sharing your thoughts and feelings can provide valuable insights and support in maintaining healthy inner boundaries.

Remember, implementing inner-personal boundaries is an ongoing process that requires self-awareness and a commitment to prioritizing your mental and emotional well-being.

Here are examples of inner-personal boundaries that may require some attention:

Self-Observation ~ Self-observation holds significance as it aligns with the practice of mindfulness and self-awareness. By observing yourself without judgment or depreciation, you can gain insight into the nature of your thoughts, emotions, and actions. Self-observation is essential as it enables you to gain insights into your thoughts, feelings, and actions to facilitate positive changes in behavior and mindset.

Through self-observation, you can cultivate mindfulness, leading to greater clarity, compassion, and the potential for breaking free from cyclical patterns of unnecessary suffering.

Reducing Stigma to Access Help ~ The stigma surrounding seeking any support and mental health care is changing, but still remains a pervasive barrier, hindering you from accessing the help you need.

Deep-seated societal misconceptions often perpetuate negative stereotypes, labeling those who seek help as weak, flawed, or even crazy. This stigma encourages a culture of silence, shaming open conversations about mental health struggles. Consequently, you may hesitate to address your problems, share your experiences, or pursue treatment due to fear of judgment and feeling like an outcast.

Seeking mental health counseling is crucial for numerous reasons. It provides a safe and confidential space for individuals to express and explore their thoughts and emotions. Mental health counselors offer valuable insights, emotional processing and support, facilitating the development of effective ways to navigate life's challenges. Counseling aids in identifying and addressing underlying issues improving inner-personal and interpersonal relationships and can teach you how to communicate more effectively and establish your healthy boundaries.

Improving Nutrition ~ A poor diet can significantly impact mental health by depriving the brain and body of essential nutrients necessary for optimal function. Diets high in processed foods, sugars, and saturated fats contribute to organ and joint inflammation and pain, and affects the brain's structure and function. Nutrient deficiencies, especially in key elements like fiber, omega-3 fatty acids, vitamins, and minerals, can impair cognitive processes, mood regulation, and increase the risk of mental health disorders.

A diet lacking in nutrient density harms the gut microbiome, influencing mental well-being through the gut-brain connection. Ultimately, a poor diet can contribute to increased stress, anxiety, depression, and chronic illnesses highlighting the intricate link between nutrition and mental health.

Foods rich in fiber, protein, and healthy fats is integral to promoting overall health and happiness. Fiber, found abundantly in fruits, vegetables, nuts, and seed, supports digestive health, regulates blood sugar levels, and contributes to a feeling of fullness, aiding in weight management. Protein, sourced from quality meats, legumes, and dairy, is essential for muscle repair, immune function, and sustained energy. Healthy fats, derived from sources like avocados, seeds, nuts, and olive oil, play a crucial role in brain health, hormone production, and maintaining cardiovascular health. Embracing a balanced diet that incorporates these vital nutrients not only supports physical health but also contributes to sustained energy levels, mental clarity, and wellness well into your senior years.

Moving Your Body ~ Moving your body is crucial for overall health, benefiting both physical and mental well-being. Regular physical activity supports cardiovascular health, maintains muscle and joint function, and contributes to a healthy weight. Engaging in movement is also linked to improved mood, reduced stress, and enhanced cognitive function. Tailoring your activity to what works best for you is essential for long-term adherence and enjoyment.

Conversely, the consequences of not moving your body can include weakened muscles, joint stiffness, weight gain, increased risk of chronic diseases, and a negative impact on mental health, such as heightened stress and reduced cognitive function. Prioritizing movement, customized to your preferences, is a proactive approach to maintaining healthy boundaries for a balanced lifestyle.

Meditation ~ Meditation holds profound importance for overall health, improving mental clarity and contentment. For individuals with attention deficit (ADD/ADHD) and chronic anxiety, meditation acts as a powerful tool to enhance focus and concentration. Regular meditation practice helps cultivate sustained attention, reduces impulsivity, and helps manage hyperactivity.

Without regular meditation, you might experience increased anxiety states, chronic physical tension, difficulty engaging with emotions, and heightened reactivity to daily stressors. Lack of mindfulness meditation practices can contribute to a scattered and overwhelmed mind, impacting your ability to focus and make clear decisions. Over time, the absence of meditation practice might hinder your ability to cultivate a deeper understanding of your thoughts and emotions, missing out on the potential for personal growth and deeply engaging with the simple joys in life.

Intentional Me Time ~ Creating time for yourself is more than just a momentary break, it is a deliberate act of building a kind and intimate relationship with yourself. This intentional solitude allows for self-reflection, self-discovery, creativity, planning, and goal setting.

In the midst of life's demands, dedicating time to connect with your own thoughts, desires, and emotions is a powerful form of self-kindness. Building an intimate relationship with yourself promotes improved interpersonal relationships and helps in navigating life's difficulties.

Social Time ~ If you are overly isolated, this can lead to a range of issues, including feelings of loneliness, anxiety, depression, and other negative impacts on mental health. Human beings are inherently social creatures, and too much social isolation can contribute to a sense of disconnection and low self-worth.

Social time is crucial for several reasons. Primarily, it provides emotional support and a sense of belonging, promoting well-being and contentment. Social interactions also offer opportunities for shared experiences, laughter, and the exchange of perspectives, enhancing overall happiness.

However, excessive social time can lead to social fatigue or burnout, characterized by feelings of exhaustion, irritability, and a reduced capacity to engage in meaningful interactions. Overcommitting to social activities may result in neglecting personal needs, leading to increased stress and a potential decline in enjoyment. Balancing social interactions with adequate time for rest, self-reflection, and individual pursuits is crucial to prevent the negative consequences associated with an overload of social engagements.

Finding Balance ~ In the juggling act of work and life, you notice things are off when feelings of discomfort, like procrastination, anxiety, and depression, start to show up. These emotions are like warning signs, telling you that the balance between your job and personal life is out of whack. It is a signal to take a step back, reassess your priorities, and make sure you're taking care of yourself. Finding the sweet spot between work and life is not only good for your mental health, but also helps keep you productive and happier in both areas.

You Are a Unique Phenomenon ~ Every human being is a unique phenomenon due to a combination of distinct experiences, perspectives, wisdom, qualities, and because you were born. It takes deep and conscious insight to begin to recognize and accept your special qualities. You have gifts and strengths that others may not be able to see from their perspective. You have an intricate blend of individual characteristics, skills, conceptual ideas, and talents that set you apart, and developing a profound connection with your soul is the key to seeing yourself in this empowering way.

Embracing Failure ~ Be patient in this process of recognizing, honoring, and implementing your boundaries. Failing at implementing boundaries is part of the process. Failure serves as a catalyst for growth by providing valuable lessons and insights. Each setback offers an opportunity to learn, adapt, and refine your approach. Embracing failure as a growth mindset means seeing setbacks as opportunities for development and maintaining a belief in the potential for progress through learning and adaptation. This mindset transforms challenges into stepping stones for accomplishing your personalized goals.

In conclusion, the implementation of both interpersonal and inner-personal boundaries plays a crucial role in fostering healthy relationships and self-care. Establishing clear boundaries in interpersonal interactions sets the foundation for respectful connections and effective communication. Simultaneously, cultivating inner-personal boundaries is pivotal for safeguarding one's mental and emotional well-being.

The delicate balance between these two dimensions is essential for maintaining a harmonious and fulfilling life. Acknowledging and honoring the need for boundaries, both external and internal, is a proactive process toward self-awareness, finding balance in life, having self-respect, and feeling empowered in navigating the complexities of relationships and personal growth.

~G~

Write about how I will communicate and my boundaries, both with yourself and others.

~ 9 ~
FAQ

Q. What if I keep crossing my boundaries? It makes me feel like a failure?

A. Continuously crossing your boundaries can lead to unkindness towards yourself, creating an ongoing deficit in self-worth and self-respect. Seeking guidance from a qualified mental health professional may be needed to help navigate and address these underlying issues.

Q. Why does setting boundaries feel so selfish to me?

A. Establishing boundaries may initially seem selfish in the face of cultural and familial norms, yet it is a vital aspect of self-care. Boundaries are not about selfishness but rather about achieving balance, attending to personal needs, and cultivating healthier relationships.

Q. How do I become kinder to myself?

A. Utilize the power of your imagination. Paint your thoughts with words as kind as a comforting embrace, just as you would speak to a loved one experiencing feelings of discouragement or emotional pain. You already possess the words have to self-soothe and uplift.

Q. How do I deal with a toxic parent that I cannot sever ties with?

A. Prioritize clarity in defining your boundaries and their consequences within your own mind before introducing them to your parent. These boundaries are set in place so you can have the most loving relationship possible while preventing chronic feelings of frustration and resentment toward them.

Q. What happens if I don't set consequences?

A. Consequences are inevitable, whether you actively define them or not. Failing to establish your interpersonal consequences often results in relational distancing and prolonged discontentment.

Q. Why am I having such a difficult time implementing my boundaries?

A. Several factors can contribute to the hesitancy in setting personal boundaries. Personal boundaries can challenge societal and familial norms, creating a sense of separation from your tribe—the people who love and care for you. Yet, it is crucial to recognize that boundaries emanate from love and compassion for both yourself and others. Boundaries are a pathway to peace, contentment, and mutual respect. Considering seeking support from a licensed mental health professional is also beneficial.

Q. What if I am afraid of the person I need to set boundaries with?

A. If you are afraid of the person you need to set boundaries with, especially in cases involving any kind of abuse or domestic violence, prioritizing your safety and well-being is paramount. Reach out to anyone who can safely support you such as friends, family, or your community organizations that specialize in domestic violence support. Seeking assistance from a crises counselor or a helpline can provide crucial guidance to help address the situation safely. Your well-being is of utmost importance, and there are resources available to support you through these challenging circumstances. The National Domestic Violence Hotline is 800-799-7233.

Q. How can I tactfully encourage someone they need to establish boundaries and suggest that they should purchase this book?

A. Initiate the conversation by sharing your positive experiences with the book and how it proved beneficial for you. Allow them to browse through your book, and if they express interest, offer to send them the link for their own copy. Remember, it is not our role to compel someone into change if they are not prepared or willing, even if it is needed. Individuals approach self-improvement with different expectations, and it is important to respect their pace for change. It is their life and therefore their consequences.

Q. Why don't other people in my life understand my need for boundaries?

A. Family members and friends may not understand your need for boundaries due to various reasons such as differing perspectives, communication styles, control issues, or a lack of awareness about the importance of personal boundaries. Open communication about your needs and reasons can facilitate a more supportive environment. However, if these efforts prove ineffective, it underscores the significance of having your clearly defined consequences in place.

Q. I am feeling overwhelmed, where do I start?

A. Start by identifying the most difficulty or emotions causing the overwhelm. Identifying your core values is a nuanced process and requires a significant amount of time and introspection. If feelings of anxiety and confusion emerge during this self-discovery journey, seeking mental health counseling can be a valuable resource. Counseling provides a supportive space to navigate the complexities hindering the identification and pursuit of personal goals. A trained professional can assist you in discovering emotional barriers while facilitating a clearer understanding of your values. This proactive step can enhance your self-confidence and contribute to a more purposeful and aligned pursuit of goals and aspirations.

~H~

Write about any comments, confusion, and questions that come to mind about setting my boundaries.

~ 10 ~
THE WRAP-UP

Establishing and maintaining boundaries is an ongoing and lifelong practice. They involve consistent attention and self-awareness to recognize and uphold your personal values and limits. As situations, relationships, and you change and evolve, you must adapt boundaries as they are a vital aspect of personal growth, healthy relationships, and your mental well-being. The journey of setting boundaries is not a one-time task, but rather a continuous process of revisiting and making necessary adaptations.

Getting yourself in a healthy and mindful place takes time and consistent effort; there is no fast solution, no magic pill. The process involves mindful self-observation, patience, and, when necessary, seeking outside assistance. Instead of looking for quick fixes, focus on small and progressive steps, permitting for and embracing setbacks. You are building a strong foundation for your improved self-worth, and this takes practice and care.

Like you, I am also a work in progress and recognize that personal growth is a lifelong practice rather than a completed state. Every experience, good and bad, is our educator, shaping us into the person we want to become. Embracing the idea that we are all a work in progress allows the freedom to evolve, make mistakes, and continually strive for improvement. It is a reminder that life is a journey of development, no matter where or what age you begin from.

Above all, consistently employ kindness and compassion towards yourself, while actively seeking joy and delight in nearly every aspect of your life.

~l~

Write about my reflections and what I have learned throughout this experience. Write any additional thoughts and ideas that arise.

ACKNOWLEDGEMENTS

This book is a heartfelt tribute to the farmers, their families, and the members of area rural communities who entrusted me to be their mental health counselor. I extend my sincere gratitude to each one of you for your trust and belief. Thank you!

I express my appreciation to **Joe** and **Erica Siler** for their steadfast dedication in diminishing the stigma around farmers seeking vital mental health treatment. Their unwavering commitment is deeply valued, and I am profoundly grateful, due to their podcast and social media content, for the honor of being acknowledged as "The Farmer's Counselor."

For additional details about the Silers and their products, visit **Yankeebeef.com**. Explore their podcast, **Full Disclosure Farming**, and find them on TikTok at **brutallyhonestAg** and **Full Disclosure Farming**.

Thank you for reading!

CATHERINE'S NEWSLETTER

Join the Community for More Transformative Experiences!

Sign up today to unlock complimentary, practice-informed, and interactive resources focused on mental well-being. Be the first to learn about Catherine's latest books and public engagements, explore insightful articles in The Wisdom Room blog, and stay updated on all things mental health by subscribing to Catherine's Newsletter.

Get valuable insights and resources delivered straight to your inbox every month! Subscribe at:

www.catherinegcleveland.com/catherines-newsletter/

To find all of Catherine's interactive books on mental health, visit:

www.catherinegcleveland.com

To learn more about mental health counseling, visit:

www.clevelandemotionalhealth.com

Connect Catherine on Social Media:

Facebook ~ Catherine G. Cleveland

LinkedIn ~ Catherine G. Cleveland

Instagram ~ @CatherineGCleveland

X (Twitter) ~ @CatherineG.Clev

TikTok ~ CatherineGCleveland

www.ingramcontent.com/pod-product-compliance
Lightning Source LLC
Chambersburg PA
CBHW080420030426
42335CB00020B/2524